Understanding
Citizenship 2

£10.99

Understanding
Citizenship 2

Second Edition

Tony Thorpe

HODDER
EDUCATION
PART OF HACHETTE LIVRE UK

INDIVIDUALS
ENGAGING IN
SOCIETY

CitizenshipFoundation

In this series we have, to the best of our knowledge, described the law as it stood on 1 January 2008. However, in trying to summarise and simplify the law we have had to leave out some legal details. Therefore, this book cannot be taken as proof of your legal rights. We strongly recommend that you seek further advice before taking any legal action.

The Citizenship Foundation is an independent educational charity, which aims to help young people to engage in the wider community through education about the law, democracy and society. It produces the Young Citizen's Passport (also published by Hodder Education), which can be used in conjunction with this book.

For further details of the work and activities of the Citizenship Foundation see the Foundation's website at www.citizenshipfoundation.org.uk, or contact The Citizenship Foundation, 63 Gee Street, London EC1V 3RS.

Telephone: (44) 020 7566 4141. Email: info@citizenshipfoundation.org.uk

The Publishers would like to thank the following for permission to reproduce copyright material: The Press Association, 8; Hulton Archive, 15 (bottom); Format 19 and 45 (bottom); Photofusion, contents page, 39; Still Pictures (Hartmut Schwarzback/Still Pictures), 46 (left); RSPCA Photolibrary © Liz Cooke, 63; Photodisc, contents page (bottom), 5 (top left), 6 (top left & bottom left), 8 (top), 9 (top, middle, bottom), 11 (top), 15 (top left), 16, 19 (top), 20 (top & bottom), 23 (middle), 25 (top), 27, 28 (left), 29 (right top middle, bottom) 31 (top right, bottom right, middle left), 41 (middle right), 43 (left) 44 (top), 45 (top left & right), 46 (top right), 47 (right), 48 (top), 49, 51 (top right), 52 (bottom left), 54 (bottom), contents page and 55, 57 (top, bottom), 59, 60 (top), 61, 62 (bottom), 63 (top & bottom); Digital Vision, contents (top), 4, 5 (top), 6 (left top & middle), 11 (top left), 24 (left); Ingram Publshing, 5 (top & right); Ikon Imaging, 43 (top left), 45 (top left); iStockphoto, 6 (bottom) 25, 31 (top right & bottom left) 53, 66; The Illustrated London News, 6 (top right), 21 (top); Punch 1901, 15 (top right); Eyewire, 21 (bottom), 52 (right); North Hertforshire District Council, 51 (bottom left & bottom right); Imageboss.com, 18 (middle left), 23 (top right), 31 (middle right & bottom left), 38 (top left), 57 (top), 58 (bottom); Associated Press, 30.

Acknowledgements: The author would like to thank Don Rowe and Jan Newton for their editorial advice and support, and Rachael Gore, Dan Mace, Nick Swinscoe, John Mitchell, Andrew Hunt, and Duncan Toms for their help in preparing and checking the text.

Every effort has been made to trace all copyright holders, but if any have been inadvertently overlooked the Publishers will be pleased to make the necessary arrangements at the first opportunity.

Although every effort has been made to ensure that website addresses are correct at time of going to press, Hodder Education cannot be held responsible for the content of any website mentioned in this book. It is sometimes possible to find a relocated web page by typing in the address of the home page for a website in the URL window of your browser.

Hachette's policy is to use papers that are natural, renewable and recyclable products and made from wood grown in sustainable forests. The logging and manufacturing processes are expected to conform to the environmental regulations of the country of origin.

Orders: please contact Bookpoint Ltd, 130 Milton Park, Abingdon, Oxon OX14 4SB. Telephone: (44) 01235 827720. Fax: (44) 01235 400454. Lines are open 9.00–5.00, Monday to Saturday, with a 24-hour message answering service. Visit our website at www.hoddereducation.co.uk

Copyright © The Citizenship Foundation 2001
First published in 2001 by
Hodder Education,
part of Hachette Livre UK,
338 Euston Road,
London
NW1 3BH.

This second edition first published (2008)

Impression number	5 4 3 2 1
Year	2013 2012 2011 2010 2009 2008

Cover photo: iStockphoto.
Design and Illustrations by Nomad Graphique.
Typeset in Garamond 3 15pt, Helvetica Neue 13pt.
Printed in Italy.

A catalogue record for this title is available from the British Library.

ISBN: 978 0340 959 190

Contents

Looking after yourself

04 Talking about sex

08 Taking precautions

10 Changing lives

Crime

14 Crimes and misdemeanours

22 Crime figures

24 Counting the cost

26 Something should be done

32 Rights and wrongs

38 Offending behaviour

Helping others

42 A helping hand

46 Rich and poor

Looking after the environment

50 Wasting away

54 Global warming

Animals

58 Animals matter

Travelling by air

64 The price of air travel

66 Influencing the future

Talking about sex

In this unit we look at the pressures on a young person over the question of underage sex.

Everybody's doing it

Sophie

'I suppose it's up to me – and Alex. We've been going out for nearly six months. I love him, and I think he loves me. We've talked about making love. Alex hasn't put any pressure on me, but I think we are both ready. I don't want Alex to think I don't want to do it, but if I leave it too long, he might go off me.

'I want to talk to my mum, but I've not been able to find the right moment. Mum knows about Alex and we've talked quite a lot about boys and relationships. I think she'd probably tell me to wait. The trouble is, I don't know how to make up my mind.'

Alex

'Of course Sophie has to decide, but I know what I think. We've been going out together for quite a while and I've had time to realise that she is really important to me.

'Most of my mates think that we are sleeping together already. I'm 17 and I've been out with loads of girls – but

I haven't "done it" yet. I've kidded along that I have because I didn't want to look stupid. In fact, I've no more experience than Sophie. I would like to talk about it, but with most lads it seems to be all about how far you can go. In fact, they make out that there's something wrong with you if you sound doubtful or worry about what might happen.

'My brother Craig is 21 and at college. He's been living with his girlfriend for a year. When mum and dad found out, they were furious. Craig knew that they would object, so he didn't tell anyone.'

Pressure

Most teenagers today probably know more about sex than their parents and grandparents did when they were their age.

Far more sex and nudity is now shown on television and in films than in the past. Sometimes the characters meet for the first time, kiss, and have sex all in the space of half an hour – without any mention or sign of contraception.

Sexual images are used in advertisements to boost the sales of almost any kind of product. Newspaper and magazine articles can also be very explicit.

This mass of sexual images can make it easy for a young person to believe that everyone – apart from them – is having sex, and that a sexual relationship could be the solution to some of their problems.

? Questions

1 How do you think Sophie and Alex should decide what to do?

2 Why do you think Alex told his friends that he'd had sexual relationships, when he hadn't? Is the pressure to have sex stronger for boys than girls – or the other way round?

3 Why do you think children and parents usually find it so difficult to talk about sex?

4 Do you think that the images of sex on television and in films affect people's attitude towards sex? Do we need new rules or laws to prevent certain things from being shown?

DESIRABLE "I NEED U"

mixes by SEX KITTEN

The law

Pressurising someone to go further than they want can reach a point where it is against the law. Kissing and touching a person without their agreement can be an assault.

In law, both people must agree to what they are doing and they must understand what is happening. A person who gets someone drunk in order to go to bed with them, or takes advantage of their drunken state, risks being charged with rape. It is also no excuse for a person accused of a sexual offence to say that they were drunk and didn't know what they were doing.

Talking about sex

Too young?

Sophie

'I know I'm not quite 15, but I don't believe that my feelings will be any different if I wait until I'm 16. Why should I have to wait? A year seems such a long time.

'Anyway, people grow up more quickly these days. Young people's bodies mature at an earlier age than they used to.

'It's my life. I think I should be able to do what I want. I've talked to my best friend, Lisa. She says I've got to do what seems right. "Take charge," she says. "Do what **you** want to do."

'My mum had her first proper boyfriend when she was 16. I don't know how far they went, but I know she would worry that I might become pregnant.'

Alex

'I'm 17, and I know Sophie's young, but most of the time she seems older than me. Girls always seem older than they are, because they mature more quickly than boys.

'I might ask my brother Craig. He'll be surprised, but I don't think he'll laugh. I think he's happy with his girlfriend Rachel and she hasn't got pregnant.

'He might come over all "big brotherly" and warn me off because of Sophie's age, but at least it would help to clear my thoughts.'

Age of consent

Sophie is below the **age of consent**. If she and Alex do decide to have sex, Alex will have broken the law and committed a criminal offence.

The age of consent in almost all parts of the UK is 16 – see the chart below for some other countries. In some countries, for example Iran and Saudi Arabia, it is unlawful for a couple who are not married to have sex.

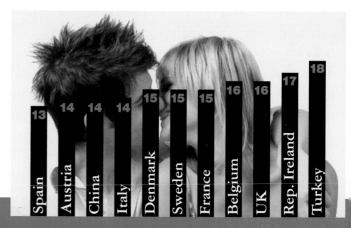

Spain	Austria	China	Italy	Denmark	Sweden	France	Belgium	UK	Rep. Ireland	Turkey
13	14	14	14	15	15	15	16	16	17	18

Power of the press

In 1875, the age of consent was raised from 12 to 13 because of worries that young girls were becoming involved in prostitution.

However, concern that young girls were being sold to brothels by their parents continued, and William Stead, a journalist, wrote a number of articles on this in a London newspaper.

In July 1885, William Stead bought 13-year-old Eliza Armstrong from her father, a chimney sweep, for £5. He did this deliberately to show how easy it was to obtain and use young girls as prostitutes. He wrote an account of what he had done in his newspaper, and was promptly arrested and charged with kidnapping a child.

The case was heard at the Old Bailey, the main criminal court in central London. William Stead was found guilty and sentenced to three months in prison. However, the trial produced so much publicity that, in the same year, Parliament raised the age of consent from 13 to 16, where it has remained.

William Stead died in 1912 on the *Titanic*, on his way to speak about world peace at an international conference in New York.

? Questions

1. What are the possible consequences of Sophie and Alex deciding whether or not to have sex?

2. How important are the views of Sophie's and Alex's parents?

3. Should the age at which people have sexual relations be decided by law? Try to explain the reasons for your view.

4. The age of consent has not changed for over 100 years. Are there any arguments for lowering the age of consent? Are there any arguments for raising it? Do you feel that the law should be changed?

The law

For boys: It is an offence for a boy or man to have sex with a girl who is under 16 years of age. The law does not recognise that a girl can consent to underage sex. From the age of ten, a boy can be charged with unlawful sex.

For girls: A girl must be 16 years old before she can legally have sex with a boy. If she is under 16, her partner is breaking the law, but she is not. Girls under 16, unlike boys, cannot be prosecuted for having sex. However, a woman over 16 who has sex with a boy under 16 may be charged with indecent assault.

KeyWords

The age of consent
The age at which a girl or boy can legally agree to sexual intercourse.

Taking precautions

In this unit we ask whether young people under 16 should be allowed to obtain contraceptive advice without the agreement of their parents.

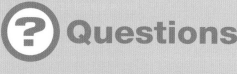

OLD ENOUGH TO DECIDE

TRUE LOVE WAITS

Victoria Gillick

Letter

It's the early 1980s. The Government is worried about the high number of pregnancies among young women. It wants to make sure that contraceptive advice and treatment is available to all young people, including those under 16.

The Government writes to doctors and family planning clinics saying that it hopes, where possible, that they would always involve the young person's parents when discussing contraception with a patient under 16. However, the letter also says that, if this is not possible, a doctor could give advice and treatment to a patient under 16 without their parents' knowledge or agreement.

Concern

Mrs Gillick is a mother of four daughters, one of whom is 15. Mrs Gillick is Roman Catholic and does not agree with the use of contraception.

Mrs Gillick strongly disapproves of the Government's action. She doesn't understand how they can allow doctors to give contraception to young people under 16, without their parents' knowledge, when the law says that they are too young to have sex.

Mrs Gillick writes to her local health authority, asking them to promise that her 15-year-old daughter will not be given contraceptive advice or treatment by medical staff without her permission. The health authority refuses.

? Questions

1 Do you think that the parent of a 15-year-old girl should have the right to decide whether or not their daughter is given contraceptive advice or treatment?

2 Should parents have the right to decide whether their children receive sex education at school?

Court

Mrs Gillick takes her case to court. It takes a long time and eventually the case is heard by the most senior judges in the country. She is defeated. By a majority of 3 to 2, the judges decide that doctors *can* give contraceptive advice and treatment to young people under 16, without the knowledge of their parents. However, this can only be done if the doctor believes that it is in the young person's best interests and that they understand what is happening.

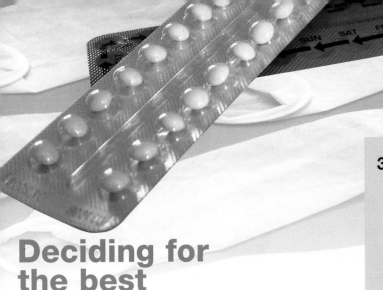

Deciding for the best

It is probably true to say that many parents would prefer their children to wait until they are adult before they have a sexual relationship.

Some will try to enforce this; others will accept that the young person will make their own choice.

Melanie

'Let's face it, kids are more knowledgeable and streetwise today. Teenagers are having sex, whether we like it or not, and I'd rather make sure that girls don't get pregnant before they are ready to have and look after a child.'

Wendy

'I was shocked when Emma asked me if she should go on the pill. She is only 15 and much too young. I said she couldn't. There are all kinds of things that could happen, which could cause both her and me great upset. It seemed to be the answer she wanted.'

3 How do you think parents should deal with their son or daughter, as far as sexual relationships are concerned? Do parents have a right to know if their son or daughter is having a sexual relationship? Should sons and daughters be treated differently?

4 Some people have argued that making contraception more easily available encourages young people to have sex. Do you agree? Try to give reasons for your answer.

The law

The law that we have today is largely a result of Mrs Gillick's case.

Anyone under 16 may be given contraceptives, as long as the doctor believes that they understand the nature and consequences of what they are doing.

The doctor can encourage the young person to tell their parents what they are doing, but cannot tell the parents without the young person's agreement.

All schools must provide sex education in a way that shows both the physical and moral issues involved. However, parents may withdraw their child from any part of the school's sex education programme that is not part of the National Curriculum even if the young person concerned is over 16.

Changing lives

Pregnancy rates amongst British teenage girls are higher than almost anywhere else in Europe. In this unit we ask why this might be and what, if anything, should be done about it.

Young love

Kerry was 15 when Naomi was born. She told no one when she realised that she might be expecting a baby. When Kerry's mother noticed that her daughter's stomach was getting larger, she asked Kerry if she was pregnant. 'Of course not,' replied Kerry, 'How could I be?'

Kerry said nothing for a while, until she was admitted to hospital with pains in her abdomen. The doctor told Kerry and her mother that she was six months pregnant.

Kerry had been with two other boys before Naomi was conceived. She said the first time she had sex it was horrible. 'I wanted to be accepted and popular at school. There's a lot of pressure on you to do it. They all said they'd had sex. Later you find out it's just talk.'

It wasn't a shock for Kerry when she realised she was pregnant. 'I knew what I was doing. We'd had sex education classes at school. I think I was too young to take it seriously. I'd wanted a baby for as long as I could remember,' she said. 'It was something that I could have and love.'

Kerry is now back in school studying for her GCSEs. She earns a small amount of money from a Saturday job and gives her **child benefit** to her mum, to help with the cost of Naomi's childminder. Kerry has not asked for any help from Ross, Naomi's father, who is a year older than Kerry. He saw his daughter not long after she was born. Since then, he has had no contact with her at all.

? Questions

1 What decisions did Kerry have to face when she realised that she was pregnant?

2 Which of these do you think was probably the most difficult?

3 Who else was affected by Kerry becoming pregnant? What do you think these people should and should not do in this situation?

4 Kerry has not asked Ross for any help. What do you think should be the responsibilities of a father in this situation?

Vital statistics

Sexual intercourse

A United Nations survey published in 2007 reported that more children in Britain had had sexual intercourse by the time they were 15 than in any other developed country. They also tended to get drunk at a much younger age.

Pregnancy

The pregnancy rate amongst young women in Britain aged 15–19 is the highest in Western Europe. Although it now appears to be falling slightly, it is twice that of Germany, and six times that of the Netherlands. It is, however, significantly lower than in the USA.

Health

In ten years, the rate of sexually transmitted diseases amongst young people under 20 has more than doubled. Some infections can cause infertility or serious complications in pregnancy and, even if treated, some are carried for life.

The law

The responsibilities that go with being a parent are automatically given to married parents and to unmarried mothers. Unmarried fathers have no rights at all over their child's upbringing without the agreement of the mother or a court order. They do, however, have responsibilities to pay towards the financial upkeep of the child.

5 In what ways can pregnancy and the birth of a child affect the lives of a teenage mother and father?

6 Why do you think the Government is so concerned about the very high rates of teenage pregnancy in England and Wales?

KeyWords

Child benefit

Money paid each week to anyone responsible for a child up to the age of 16 (or 18 if in full-time education).

Finding an answer

With newspaper reports of boys and girls as young as 11 or 12 becoming parents, the Government wants to find ways of persuading young people not to have sex at such an early age. How might this be done?

Here are some ideas.

Better sex education

All schools in England and Wales must, by law, teach some form of sex education. This must pay attention to moral issues as well as the biological details of conception and pregnancy.

Some schools provide a very good sex education programme for their pupils. In others, however, not all teachers are trained to deal with the subject properly. They may be embarrassed to answer certain questions and it can be difficult to talk about personal issues in a class of 30 people.

THINK! Should it be the job of schools, rather than parents, to give sex education to young people?

Help people find success

Teenage pregnancy rates tend to be higher in places of high unemployment and poverty. In this situation, having a baby can represent some kind of achievement to someone who does not have much hope of getting the things that many other people have.

It is believed that if young women can find more success in their lives, they will value themselves more and will be more likely to make sure they don't become pregnant until they feel ready for motherhood.

THINK! What sort of things make people feel more successful?

Say no

Some people argue that sex outside marriage is morally wrong, and that the best way to avoid teenage pregnancy is to wait until you are married before having sex.

Some of the organisations promoting abstinence avoid giving advice on contraception, believing that to do so would suggest that it is OK to have sex.

Talk more

Parents should talk to their children about sex and feelings much more than they do. They shouldn't leave sex education to schools or to their children's friends.

THINK! Do children want to talk with their parents about sex?

Do you agree that sex outside marriage is wrong?

Excessive drinking

It is believed that alcohol has a strong effect on the sexual behaviour of women. A 2007 report indicated that four out of ten sexually active 13–14 year olds were drunk when they first had sex.

(!) THINK! Should more efforts be made to stop teenagers buying alcohol?

Take away benefits

Some people argue that teenage girls sometimes deliberately have a child in order to receive Government benefits and support.

Several American states have cut the benefits available to young, single women with children. Where these measures have been introduced, the number of teenage pregnancies has fallen.

(!) THINK! Is there any way of really knowing if people have children in order to receive Government benefits?

Some parents find it difficult to talk to their children about sex. Why is this?

Emergency contraception

Emergency contraception can prevent pregnancy if taken within 72 hours of unprotected sex. It is available free, whatever a person's age, from doctors, family planning clinics, most NHS walk-in centres and some hospital emergency departments. It may also be bought from a chemist by someone aged 16 or over.

IN CASE OF EMERGENCY

BREAK GLASS

Experienced school nurses in a small number of schools in England and Wales also offer emergency contraception and sexual health advice.

(!) THINK! Some people argue that emergency contraception encourages people to have sex at too young an age. Do you agree?

(?) Questions

1 Write down what you think are the strengths and weaknesses of each idea for reducing the number of teenage pregnancies. Can you see any difficulties in putting any of them into practice?

2 What advice would you give to the Government about reducing the number of teenage pregnancies?

In this unit we ask why certain actions are a crime, and others are not.

Mission impossible

Right now, Zak should be at school in Mrs Taylor's maths lesson, not walking along the road, in the rain, having just been thrown off a bus.

Zak's little sister, Naina, lives five miles away with their mum. It is Naina's birthday today and Zak wanted to make sure that she knew he had not forgotten. He had bought her a present and decided to give it to her before she left for school.

Zak left home early, telling his dad that he was calling for a friend. Instead, he caught the bus to Naina's house. He didn't have the fare, but just flashed his pass hoping the driver would think that he was on his way to school. The bus was full and, although Zak got a seat, several people were standing. One was a woman who was heavily pregnant. He could feel the pressure from the other passengers who were asking, 'Why isn't that boy giving up his seat?'

He gave the present to his little sister. Their mum had already left for work. Zak walked Naina to her school and then waited at the bus stop for the journey back.

When it came, the bus was almost empty. Zak sat down and rested his feet on the seat opposite. An inspector got on and took a look at his pass. 'You can't use that,' he said, 'it's for another route. The fare is £2.20.' Zak swore, without realising what he was saying. He had meant it more in astonishment than anger. From then on he had no chance. At the next stop he was turned off, which is why he is walking along the road, in the rain.

? Questions

1 Draw up a list of the things that Zak did that you think were wrong.

2 Now put a mark or line under those things that you think might have been against the law.

3 This will probably leave some items on your list that are not marked. Why are they wrong if they are not against the law?

Moral or criminal?

You probably thought that some, but not all, of the things that Zak did were against the law. This is because not everything that we think is wrong is actually against the law. It's not against the law to cheat in a game of tennis, but most people would say that it is wrong. Cheating in games is one of the many things that are against the rules of how to behave in our society (and many other societies too). 'Morality' is a word sometimes used to describe these rules of conduct. Often, morality and law stand for exactly the same thing. Most people believe that it is morally wrong to break in and steal from someone's house. This is also against the law.

However, people do not always believe that the law is right. In fact, sometimes it may be completely wrong.

Bad law

In the 1930s the Nazi Government in Germany passed many laws that treated Jewish people very badly. From 1933, Jews could not go to the cinema or theatre. In 1935, they lost the right to vote.

Michael Siegal, a Jewish lawyer, is forced to wear a sign which reads, 'I am a Jew, I will never again complain about the Nazis.'

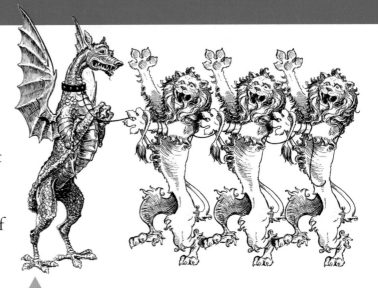

Other examples of wrong law are those that were passed by the English against the Welsh in the 16th century. Welsh people could not hold important positions in their own country nor could they charge an English person with a crime.

4 Let's now look more closely at the connection between morality and crime.

a) Try to think of another example of something:
   • that you think is wrong and is also against the law
   • that is wrong, but not against the law
   • that is against the law, but is not wrong apart from this.

   In each case write down why you think that the action you describe is right or wrong.

b) What happens when you break a moral rule? What happens when you break a legal rule?

c) Who enforces moral rules? Who enforces legal rules?

5 If you had the chance to change just one of the laws that you have mentioned, what would it be and why?

Crimes and misdemeanours

Right or wrong?

A little extra

Every month, John Elliot put a small part of his wages into a savings account in his bank. It wasn't much, but it was the only way he could save enough money for a holiday with his family.

Each month, the bank sent John a statement telling him how much he had in his account.

When the statement for the month of April arrived, John saw that he had more money in his account than he had expected – £20,000 more, in fact. John phoned the bank to say that there had been a mistake.

'No,' said the person John spoke to, 'everything is in order. The money is yours.'

Mystified as to where the extra cash had come from, John wrote a letter to the bank pointing out that the money was not his.

Again the bank said that they had double-checked the account and that no mistake had been made. John still wasn't happy. He decided to try once more and wrote to the bank for a second time. Again he was told that the money was his.

Although John was certain that a mistake had been made, he knew that the extra money would come in useful. Shortly afterwards, he decided to buy a new sofa and then, a couple of weeks later, started to redecorate his house.

He then thought that it would be a good idea to go away with his family while the house was being painted. He booked a fortnight's holiday to Greece.

A month after his return, John had a call from the bank. They had discovered that someone with the same name as John had paid the money into the bank and that the money had been put into John's account by mistake.

The bank asked for their money back, and John gave them what he had left – a little over £9,000. The bank decided to inform the police and, after a short investigation, John was charged with theft.

1 Put yourself in the position of a member of the jury who has to decide whether or not the evidence shows that John has committed theft.

To help you with this, look at the legal definition of theft under **The law** heading below.

You need to answer three questions: did John:
- behave dishonestly?
- take something from someone else?
- intend to keep the money?

If you decide that the answer to all of these questions is 'yes', then John should be found guilty of theft.

2 Did John do anything in this case that was morally wrong? Try to explain your answer.

Owning up

All of us have, at some time, found ourselves in a position that is similar to John's, in finding, or being given, something that is not really ours. How should we deal with these situations? What should we do?

3 Look at the following examples and decide what you think the person in each case should do. Also try to work out what the law says about each one.

- **Cara** gets out of her mum's car in a multi-storey car park and picks up a £1 coin she sees on the floor.

- **Janaki** is waiting to use the cash machine outside the bank, which is closed. The person using the machine in front of her takes his card and receipt, but forgets to pick up his cash. Janaki counts out £60 in £10 notes.

- **Sunita** pays for a drink and cake in a café with a £5 note. The assistant is busy and gives Sunita £7.50 change. Sunita immediately sees the mistake.

- **Phil** takes his car to the garage for a new stereo to be fitted and collects the car at the end of the day. A few days later he discovers an expensive set of spanners underneath the front seat. He is certain that they belong to someone at the garage.

The law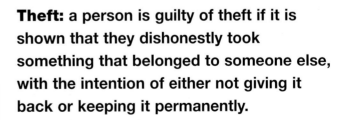

Theft: a person is guilty of theft if it is shown that they dishonestly took something that belonged to someone else, with the intention of either not giving it back or keeping it permanently.

It is an offence to keep something that you find, unless you have good reason to believe it is not possible to discover who the owner is.

Crimes and misdemeanours

What is a crime?

This seems an easy question to answer. Most people would say that a crime is something that is against the law. That is absolutely true. However, not everything that is against the law is a crime. For example, the boss who gives an employee the sack without good reason isn't committing a crime, but is breaking the law.

Scene of crime?

All of these situations are against the law, but not all of them are crimes.

A Returning home by taxi after a night out together, a woman realises her husband is unwell and in great pain. Although she has had several glasses of wine, she decides to drive him to the hospital.

B A man parks his car on double yellow lines while he gets some money out of the cash machine.

C A surgeon makes a mistake in carrying out a difficult operation. The patient suffers brain damage that affects her for the rest of her life.

D A man leaves a supermarket with two pork pies in his pocket, which he does not intend to pay for.

E A passenger refuses to switch off her mobile phone as she flies on a British aircraft to Paris.

F Two people take a short cut on private land across a farmer's field.

G As they leave the ground, a crowd of football fans starts to shout racist insults at a group of black people.

H A couple complain that their hotel is of a much lower standard than the one they were promised. The holiday company refuses to return any of the money the couple have paid.

? Questions ?

1 Four of the cases A–H are crimes. Which do you think they are?

2 Which are the two most serious cases in the list? Which are the two least serious? Give reasons for your choices.

3 Are crimes always the most serious cases?

Criminal or civil?

Most of our law is divided into two categories: *criminal law* and *civil law*.

Criminal law covers behaviour that is thought to be so serious that the police take on the job of investigating the offence. With enough evidence, the police will charge the suspect and the case will go to court.

If the person is found guilty, the court will decide on a punishment – possibly a fine or period of imprisonment. Theft, assault and murder are all crimes.

Civil laws are laws designed to settle arguments or disagreements between individuals or groups of people. These are not dealt with by the police.

For example, a boss who sacks a group of workers because they want to join a trade union isn't committing a crime, but the workers would probably want their jobs back or compensation for the loss of work.

Civil laws give the workers the right to have their case heard at a special hearing, known as an employment tribunal, which decides whether they have been treated

was it you?

was it you?

unfairly. If it finds that they have, it will probably order the boss to pay the workers money in compensation.

Prove it!

There are many different kinds of law court, but they all tend to be places where evidence is heard from both sides and a decision is reached about whether the law has been broken, who is responsible, and what should happen to the people concerned.

The level of proof required in courts that hear criminal cases is much greater than for civil cases. The guilt of someone accused of a crime, such as assault, must be proved *beyond reasonable doubt*.

A civil court reaches a verdict on the *balance of probabilities*. A person who feels that they have been wrongly sacked from work must show that there is a strong probability that they have lost their job unfairly.

THINK! Why do you think that courts require a higher level of proof in criminal cases?

All change

The way of the world

- In England and Wales, it is against the law for one person to marry another if either is already married to someone else. In a small number of countries such as Morocco and Libya, however, this is allowed.

- In Saudi Arabia, it is against the law for anyone to buy alcohol. In England and Wales, alcohol may be bought from anywhere with a licence to sell it by anyone aged 18 or over.

- In Australia, anyone who is able to vote but chooses not to, commits a crime and is punished with a small fine. It is also an offence in

Australia to leave your car keys in your car.

- In the United States, it is illegal to overtake a school bus that has stopped to allow children to get off.

- The sale, import and possession of chewing gum is forbidden in Singapore. Anyone breaking this law may be fined.

? Questions

1 What do these statements show you about the nature of law?

The way we were

Many of our laws have altered over the last 40 years. Here are just a few of the changes.

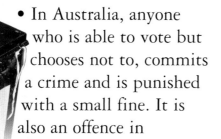

1961 Suicide is no longer an offence.

1967 Abortion, under certain conditions, becomes legal.

1967 Homosexuality between men, in private, is no longer an offence.

1969 The death penalty is abolished for murder.

1975 Discrimination against someone because of their sex becomes illegal.

1976 It becomes unlawful to discriminate against someone in employment and education because of their race.

1986 It becomes an offence to stir up racial hatred.

1994 It is no longer illegal for shops to open on Sundays.

The way we were

f we go further back into the past we find xamples of laws and punishment that seem articularly unfair today.

Until the end of the 18th century the law allowed men and women to be kept in England and Wales as slaves. In 1772, there were an estimated 10,000 slaves in England.

In 1776, there were 160 offences in England and Wales that were punishable by death. There was probably no other country in the world, at the time, where so many crimes carried the death penalty.

- In 1801, anyone caught stealing anything worth more than a shilling could be executed. A 13-year-old boy was hanged for breaking into a house and stealing a spoon. Two sisters aged eight and eleven suffered the same fate in 1808 and, in the same year, 13 people were hanged for being in the company of gypsies.

It is difficult today to understand how the law and the legal system could treat people in such a way. And it is hard to imagine what our decendants will think in 200 years' time when they look back on the 21st century.

1995 Disabled people are given some protection against discrimination at work.

1998 A new law requires all public bodies, such as the courts, police, schools and hospitals, to protect people's human rights.

2 Can you name any other changes in the law over the last 40 years? Do you feel that these changes are for the better or the worse?

3 Why do you think the law changes?

4 Can you think of any law that will have to change over the next 200 years? Which old laws might we get rid of and what new laws might we need to pass?

Crime figures

In this unit we look at some of the difficulties involved in working out how much crime takes place in our society.

The statistics

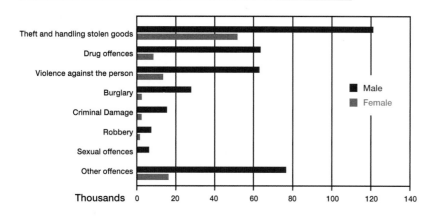

Trends in recorded crime
(Source: Crime in England and Wales 2006/07, Home Office)

Offenders as a percentage of the population: by age, 2004, England and Wales (Source: Home Office)

People found guilty or cautioned for indictable offences in 2004

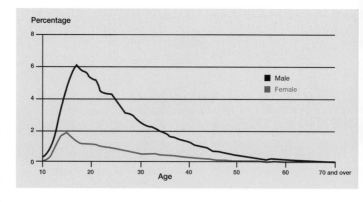

Questions

1 Look at the graphs of crime statistics. For each one, write down at least two things that you can see from the figures.

2 Do these raise any questions in your mind about patterns of crime in Britain? If so, what are they?

Reporting restrictions

Most of the information that the police have about crime comes from the general public. Without this help, the police could do very little. The police discover relatively little crime entirely by themselves. Out of every five crimes known to the police, four are reported by members of the public.

Sometimes, crime figures are affected by things that have nothing to do with crime itself. During the 1980s many more people had phones installed in their homes, which made crimes easier to report. More people also started to insure their property against loss or theft, which meant that if they wanted to claim for something that was stolen, they had to tell the police.

Crime figures can also be influenced by changes in technology. During the 1990s the police fitted automatic cameras on many more stretches of road. In 1993, the roadside cameras detected just over 30,000 motoring offences. By 1997, this figure had increased to almost 340,000, and in 2006 it was reported to be more than two million.

But what about the crimes that are not known to the police? How much crime goes unreported?

• **Silent witness:** 'I saw the man just take the book off the shelf, tuck it inside his coat and then leave. I don't suppose the shop will even realise, and the police would never find him.'

• **Home truths:** 'I know he shouldn't hit me, but I couldn't call the police.'

• **Tax free:** 'I do a bit of work on the side. Last year I cleared almost £8,000 in this way. I get the money and the customer gets a good job for half the price. We don't want the taxman involved as well.'

3 Draw up a list of the sort of crimes that you think might not be known to the police.

4 In what kinds of situations might it be difficult for a member of the public to report a crime to the police?

Telling the tale

There are other ways in which crime can be measured, which, experts say, produce a more accurate picture of crime.

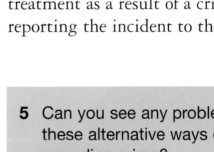

Have you COMMITTED, WITNESSED or been a VICTIM of a CRIME?

TALK TO US!

One is to ask people to speak privately about the crimes that they themselves have committed. Another is to ask people about crime that has affected them, as victims. A third method is to look at the records of casualty departments in hospitals. Quite often a person goes to hospital for treatment as a result of a crime, without reporting the incident to the police.

5 Can you see any problems with these alternative ways of recording crime?

6 Do you think that people should be required by law to report a crime?

7 It has been suggested that hospitals could inform the police if they suspect that a patient has been injured as a result of a crime. What would be the effects of this? Do you think that it would be a good or bad thing?

Counting the cost

In this unit we look at some of the ways in which crime affects our society.

Where's the harm?

Doing the rounds

'Some days a friend and I would go round offices, cafés and pubs looking for bags and jackets left unattended.

'If a door was left open, we knew what to do. If anyone stopped us, we would just make up a name and pretend that we were looking for someone.

'People say "don't you think of the victim?" but I don't. I think of myself first. There's £50 in it for me. I don't think of the person and how they are going to get home tonight without any money. There's no feeling of guilt, though if I started thinking about the person I probably would feel bad.

I'm not into robberies and muggings because I'm not into harming anyone at the end of the day.'

Gary, aged 20, from London.

❓ Questions

1 Gary admits to committing hundreds of crimes: shoplifting, breaking into cars and receiving stolen goods. He's been warned, fined and sent to a prison for young offenders. He says that he doesn't think about the consequences of what he does.

What do you think are the effects of Gary:
- taking someone's wallet
- smashing a car window and taking the stereo
- making dodgy coins for drinks, cigarette and ticket machines?

2 Gary says that he is not into harming anyone. Do you agree? Try to explain what you feel.

Damage

Bridget let herself into her house and walked into the front room. The scene was absolute devastation. Things all over the floor, lights smashed, chairs upturned. It was impossible to recognise the room that she had left an hour before. It was the same upstairs. They'd been through everything, even her clothes.

Bridget rang the police. While she waited for them to come, she rang a friend, to tell her what had happened.

'How dare they come to my house and go through my things' she said. 'It wasn't as if I've got much in the first place.'

'I don't know if I really want them to find my stuff,' Bridget went on, 'not after someone else has used it like that.'

Bridget eventually managed to piece together the losses: a CD player, money, microwave, leather coat, passport, driving licence, and a ring given to her by her grandmother.

The police managed to find the people responsible. They were in a road accident. When the police checked their car they found, among other things, Bridget's ring and passport.

Bridget hates the house now, but she can't afford to move. She doesn't like being there alone and worries that someone will break in again.

3 Apart from the value of the goods and money that have been stolen, what are the effects of crimes like this?

4 What do you think is the worst thing about crime in our society?

The cost of crime

A recent news report stated that Britain spends more on law and order per person than any other country in the Western world.

The costs of crimes like theft include those of the police, courts and lawyers; the cost of treatment or a prison sentence; plus the costs to the victim – replacing the goods, time off work, and possibly shock and illness.

Less crime

Most people would say that it would be impossible to have a society without crime, because people will always, for some reason, break the law. But what if we had less crime? What difference would it make?

THINK! Imagine that property or violent crime fell by 50 per cent over the next five years. What benefits would this bring to people's lives?

Something should be done

In this unit we look at some of the causes of crime and ask who has responsibility for lowering the crime rate.

Crime concern

Most people would probably agree that some crimes are worse than others.

Driving at 75 mph on the motorway

Driving a car or motorcycle on the road without road tax

Drinking alcohol in a pub at 16

Laying a large piece of metal across a railway track

Breaking into a house and stealing a person's property

Making a copy of a CD for a friend

Deliberately not paying tax

Driving when over the permitted alcohol limit

Deliberately treating an animal cruelly

Smoking marijuana

Stealing from a shop

Attacking and robbing someone in the street

❓ Questions

1 All these situations are crimes. Which of them do you think are wrong:
   • in every case
   • in some cases
   • never?

2 Look at the actions that you decided were wrong in *every* case. Why are they wrong? Do they share any qualities or characteristics that make them always wrong?

3 Now look at those actions that you thought were *sometimes* wrong. Why are they not as serious as those you thought were *always* wrong?

4 Why do you think the situations that you feel are not wrong are categorised as crimes?

A family friend

When 87-year-old Edith Campbell went to open the door of her flat, she was expecting a visit from the hairdresser. Instead she faced two figures, wearing black clothes and balaclavas, who knocked her down and kicked her as she lay on the floor.

The thieves stole £800 from Mrs Campbell, along with her bank card and pension book, all of which were hidden behind the bathroom sink.

Shortly after the attack, the two people responsible

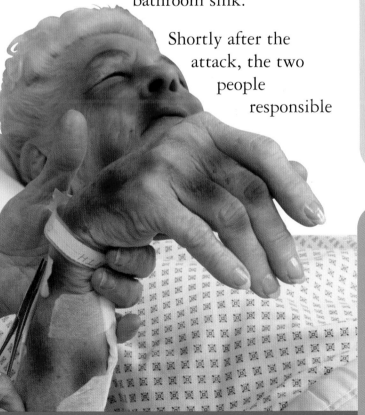

went to a pub and were heard boasting about what they had done. One of their friends went to the police.

Edith Campbell was found by a neighbour and taken to hospital with broken ribs and severe bruising to her face and body. Five days later she died.

The police arrested two sisters, aged 17 and 19. In court, they were found guilty of robbery and **manslaughter**. They had known Mrs Campbell for some time. She had given them birthday cards and presents when they were children and, on an earlier occasion, had told them where she kept her money.

5 What are your reactions to this case? What words would you choose to describe your feelings?

6 What did the two young women do that was wrong?

7 Was their friend right to go to the police? Try to give a reason for your answer.

8 What might explain why this crime took place?

KeyWords

Manslaughter

Deliberately killing another person is normally seen as murder, but there are times when death occurs without the person responsible knowingly intending it to happen. This is called manslaughter and normally carries a lighter sentence than murder.

Something should be done

Trying to understand

Not all bad

Crimes such as the attack on Edith Campbell, described on the previous page, are tragic for all those involved. Most people find it difficult to understand why or how she could have been attacked in this way.

Despite people's fears of crime, we don't live in a society full of vicious thugs and hooligans. Violent crime makes up only six per cent of recorded crime, and much of this takes place between people who know one another.

Most crimes are offences against property, such as theft and burglary, and most of these are committed by a relatively small number of people. About five per cent of offenders commit about 70 per cent of all the property crime. As we have seen already, young men (aged 15–25) commit most of the crimes that are known to the police.

THE CAUSES

For many years, people have tried to understand why people commit crimes. Here are some explanations that have been put forward for some of the crimes that *young* people commit.

People commit crimes because:
- they are born criminal – it's in their genes
- they let themselves be influenced by other people
- they were given little care and love when they were children
- they are poor and live in bad conditions
- fighting and theft are thought to be good things in the area where they live
- they drink too much
- people sometimes look up to those who break the law
- they don't have a very high opinion of themselves, and don't really care if they get into trouble.

look dad!!

mmmm great!

...OF CRIME...

BIG GANGSTER
MOVIE
Starring big ron

Victims and Witnesses

Justine: 'I'd been at work all day and left the car in the multi-storey car park. I unlocked the door and got in. I didn't realise there was anything wrong. I started the engine and I put my hand down to turn on the radio. It wasn't there. Someone had stolen it. Then I saw the glass all over the back seat.'

Errol: 'Two lads who got off the train before me jumped over the ticket barrier and then walked straight out of the station! It really annoys me when people don't pay their fare. Where's the justice?'

Wajid: 'I was late leaving school and took a short cut to the bus stop. These two big lads stopped me and started pushing me around. They wanted some money. They cracked me a couple of times in the face, but I managed to get away. I was still shaking when I got home.'

❓ Questions

1 Read through each point on the panel opposite. Are there any explanations that you think are wrong and would reject straight away? Try to explain why.

2 Take each of the explanations that you agree with and suggest a situation or circumstance in which it might apply.

3 Look at the three crimes described above and try to suggest a reasonable explanation why each one might have been committed.

4 The Government has said that it wants to deal with the causes of crime. Pick three points from the list on page 28 and suggest what could be done to reduce the part they play in causing crime.

Something should be done

Getting involved

A duty to help?

In the early hours of 31 August 1997, radio and television stations all over the world reported the news of the death of Diana, Princess of Wales, in a car accident in Paris.

After dining together, the Princess and her friend Dodi Fayed left the Hotel Ritz in a chauffeur-driven car. As they drove away they were pursued by photographers in cars and on motorcycles hoping to get a picture of the Princess and her companion.

The vehicles sped through the centre of the city and headed into an underpass alongside the River Seine. There, the Mercedes-Benz in which the Princess was travelling careered out of control and smashed into one of the tunnel pillars.

The police were called, but it was the photographers who were among the first to reach the accident. However, several witnesses later said that some of these people did not help to deal with the injured, concentrating instead on taking pictures and then leaving, to get the photographs to the newspapers as quickly as possible.

In France, it is a criminal offence for a person not to help someone in danger – unless they would be put in danger themselves. After the accident, an investigation was held to decide whether there was enough evidence to show that any of the photographers had broken the law in this way. Eventually it was decided that there was not, and no one was charged with an offence.

? Questions

1 Can you suggest reasons why people *should* help in this situation? What sort of help might they give? Are there any reasons why they should *not* help?

2 Should Britain have a law making it an offence not to help someone in danger?

Going it alone

Much of the information used in the detection of crime comes from the general public. Someone who has suffered an attack or a burglary will probably want the offender to be caught and dealt with as quickly as possible, and will usually help the police as much as they can.

But what about the person who is not directly involved? What is our responsibility when we know about or see a crime being committed, but are not directly affected? Should we get involved or is there a stronger argument that says we should not?

3 Look at the situations described on this page, and decide what you think the people involved should do in each case.

4 In which case do you think it is most important that the person should act? Try to explain why.

• **Gareth** works in the kitchens of a large hospital and knows that one of the people with whom he works is taking food from the store. On some occasions, Gareth has seen the man load boxes of biscuits and cakes from the kitchen straight into his car.

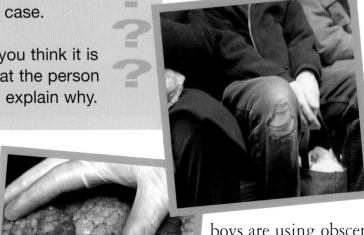

• **Euan and Ruth** are sitting on a crowded train when two of the passengers start to argue, and a fight breaks out.

• Three nights ago, there was a fire at **Lydia's** school and the sports hall was badly damaged. Basketball, badminton, football and gymnastics have all been cancelled until further notice. Lydia is 95 per cent certain that she knows the name of the person responsible – a student in her year group.

• **Sarfraz**, who is in his 30s, is waiting at a bus stop with three other people. Two of them are boys, aged 10–12. The third is an elderly man. The boys are using obscene language and the old man is clearly upset.

• **Dalton** works as a window cleaner. One day, a customer offers to sell him some very cheap whisky and gin. The customer makes a good living selling large quantities of cigarettes and alcohol that have either been stolen or smuggled into Britain from France.

5 What kinds of things sometimes stop people from reporting crime or criminals to the police? Are these good reasons, or bad?

Rights and wrongs

In this unit we look at how a young person suspected of committing a criminal offence is treated by the police and courts.

In the bag

Vijay: 'It was about 3.30 in the afternoon. I'd been in the café for a few minutes when I noticed that the two young lads sitting at another table were arguing. One of them had a carrier bag, which the other tried to grab. Making his escape, the boy with the bag stood up and ran through the door marked "Toilets". The other boy followed close behind.

'Voices were raised and I heard what sounded like someone being pushed against the wall. The owner of the café went to the door, opened it and told the boys to get out.

They took no notice and she was back in a second saying that she was calling the police.

'I felt that I ought to do something. I opened the door to the toilets and saw the two boys exchanging punches. They looked about 14 years old. I grabbed the taller boy with one hand and with the other tried to hold the smaller lad at arm's length.

'They both shouted at me to let go, but whenever I did they began fighting again. I tried to find out what the problem was. The smaller boy said that his mate had taken some money that belonged to him and that he wanted it back.

'Suddenly the bigger boy, who now had hold of the bag, slipped my grasp and ran out of the door. A minute or so later, he was back, held firmly by two police officers.'

PC Jarrett: 'My colleague and I were on patrol in the High Street when we received a call saying that two youths were fighting in a café nearby. Just as we were approaching the entrance a young person ran out of the door. I gave chase, caught him, and brought him back to the building. In the process he kicked and punched me in an effort to escape.'

> **!**
> **THINK!**
> **What do you think the police officers should do now?**

PC James: 'I asked both boys for their name, age and address. The younger boy said he was Daniel Simpson and that he was 13 years old. He gave me his address and the name of his school.

'The older boy said his name was Mark Lyddon. He also gave me his address and said that he was 14 and went to the same school as Daniel.'

PC Jarrett: 'I looked in the carrier bag that Mark had been holding and found that it contained two men's shirts, two T-shirts, a couple of disposable cameras and four unopened packs of batteries.

'I asked Mark Lyddon who the property belonged to. He said it was his and that he had bought the items in various shops that afternoon.'

> **!**
> **THINK!**
> **What choices do the police officers now have?**
>
> **What do you think they should do?**

PC Jarrett: 'We decided to **arrest** both boys for causing an **affray** and to take them to the police station. If it had been earlier (it was now just after 4p.m.) we might have taken them both back to school.

'Both boys were searched at the station, and £30 was found in Mark Lyddon's pocket.'

> **!**
> **THINK!**
> **Draw up a list of the questions that you think the police would probably want to ask Daniel and Mark.**
>
> **How should Daniel and Mark be treated by the police? What rights should the boys be given, and why?**

Key**Words**

Affray
A disturbance, such as an argument or fight, between two or more people in a public place.

Arrest
Taking away a person's freedom to go where they please. Someone arrested by the police cannot normally be held for more than 24 hours without being charged with a crime.

Rights and wrongs

At the police station

Caution

After the police have arrested someone who is under 17, they must ask the parents to come to the police station before the young person is questioned any further.

If the young person's mum or dad can't come, the police must ask another adult, such as a relative or friend, to attend. If none of these is available, the police will arrange for someone else, such as a social worker, to be present. This person is called 'an appropriate adult'.

 THINK! Why do you think the law says that an appropriate adult must be with a young person when they are questioned by the police?

Mark's mother and Daniel's father reach the police station about an hour after the boys' arrest. They are told by the police of their right to have a solicitor present when their sons are questioned. Both parents agree, and the police call a **duty solicitor** for each of the boys.

 THINK! Why do you think a person is allowed to have a solicitor with them when they are being questioned at the police station?

When the duty solicitors arrive, they each speak separately to Mark and Daniel, doing their best to make sure that the boys understand what is happening.

The police question Mark first, and then Daniel. The interview is tape-recorded and each boy has their parent and solicitor in the room with them. Before they begin, the police explain that anything said in the interview may be used in court.

The story

Mark: 'We bunked off school and went into town. We bought a few things for presents. I don't remember the names of the shops and I don't have the receipts because I threw them away.

'We got into an argument in the café about some money, which Danny said I owed him. It wasn't serious.

'I ran because I got scared when the woman said she would call the police. I didn't mean to kick the police officer. It was an accident. I didn't know what I was doing.'

Daniel: 'Mark and I took all the stuff. We've done it before. I distracted the assistant while Mark put the things in his bag.

'He doesn't always pay me when we sell it. That's what the fight was about. Half of the money was mine.'

PC James: 'I checked Daniel's story. One of the shops that he said they had visited has security cameras. The tape shows the boys entering and leaving the shop but it is not clear whether they stole anything.

'I also checked police records and found that neither boy has a criminal record.'

Next steps

The police now have to decide what to do next. In this case, they have three choices:

1   Let Daniel and Mark go, without charging them with any offence.

2   Give each boy either a reprimand or a final warning. However, these can only be given if the person admits the crime and has no previous convictions. The police must also feel that it is better that the person concerned does not appear in court.

3   Charge both Daniel and Mark with one or more offences.

 THINK! Which of these three alternatives would you advise the police to take? Give reasons for your answer.

Charge

The police decide to charge both boys with theft and causing an affray. They also charge Mark with assaulting a police officer.

Mark and Daniel are told that their case will be heard in court in three days' time. The police must allow them to go home on **bail**, unless there is a good reason not to.

 THINK! For what reasons would it be reasonable for the police not to grant bail? Should the police grant Mark and Daniel bail?

Key**Words**

Bail
A person given bail is allowed to go home, but must promise to appear in court or at a police station when they are told to do so.

Duty solicitor
Someone who is being interviewed by the police at a police station can ask to see the duty solicitor. This is a lawyer who will give free legal advice to the person being questioned.

Rights and wrongs

In court

Not long to wait

Mark and Daniel are both given bail. But, meanwhile, they must go to school and report to the **youth court** in three days' time for their trial.

Friday morning

Daniel and Mark arrive separately at the court building with their parents. The duty solicitors that they saw at the police station will speak on behalf of each boy in court. While they are waiting for their case to be called, each boy talks to his solicitor.

Mark says that he has decided to plead guilty. He says that he has changed his mind because he was scared when the police caught him.

In court

Daniel and Mark go into court with their parents. The charges are read out and each boy is asked if he pleads guilty or not guilty. Mark and Daniel both plead guilty.

The three **magistrates** are told that neither boy has any previous convictions.

They must then listen to the **Crown Prosecutor**, who gives the main details of the case, and then to Daniel's and Mark's solicitors, who speak in their defence.

Crown Prosecutor: 'On the afternoon of 2 October the two boys stole items from several shops to the value of £87.92.

'At about 3.30p.m. the boys bought a drink at a town centre café. There they had a disagreement, which led to a fight.

'The café owner then called the police and the boys were arrested. Mark Lyddon tried to escape, and in doing so, kicked one of the officers several times.'

Defence: 'Mark wishes to say to the court that he is sorry for what he did. He realises that he should not have stolen from the shops, nor have kicked the police officer.

'Mark has found difficulty in dealing with his parents' recent separation. He has spent little time at home and has been led by others into missing school and stealing.

'Daniel Simpson moved to this area a year ago when his father changed jobs. Until then he had not been in trouble with the police. He did not settle well in his new school and has been bullied. His parents believe that this led him to miss school and get into trouble.'

Decision

The magistrates must now decide how they will sentence Daniel and Mark.

 THINK! What do you think should be the purpose of the punishment that the magistrates give?

The magistrates decide to do three things:

1   To give both Mark and Daniel a Referral Order. In Daniel's case, for five months, and in Mark's, for seven.

Under the Referral Order, Mark and Daniel will be required to attend a Youth Offender Panel, made up of two trained volunteers from the local community and a member of the **Youth Offending Team**. The Panel will try to find out the reasons for each boy's criminal behaviour and to make an agreement (or contract) with both the boys and their parents on how to stop similar things happening again.

If Mark and Daniel do not keep to this agreement, their case will be referred back to court for re-sentencing.

2   As Mark is under 16, his parents are ordered to pay PC Jarrett £50 in compensation for her injuries.

3   They also give each boy's parents a Parenting Order. This means that the parents will be given help in trying to make sure their children behave and go to school. If the parents do not keep to this Order they can be fined up to £1,000.

 THINK! What do you think of these measures? Do they do the job that you think they ought to?

Is it right to involve Daniel and Mark's parents in their punishment? Explain the reasons for your answer.

KeyWords

Crown Prosecutor
The lawyer who presents the case in court against someone charged with a criminal offence.

Magistrates
Members of the local community who are trained to listen to and deal with all the different kinds of cases that come to magistrates' and youth courts.

Youth Court
A special court only dealing with children and young people ages 10–17.

Youth Offending Team
A group of people who try to stop young people from offending. The team includes social workers, and police and probation officers.

Offending behaviour

In this unit we ask how a young person who has committed a crime should be treated.

Criminal damage

Over the top

Lance (14) and his two friends Brett (14) and Greg (12) have been taken to the police station for questioning.

The boys were seen behind their old primary school on the night that four large windows in the building were broken. A door was also damaged and a waste paper bin set on fire.

The police spoke to each of the boys at home, with their parents present. They told them that they had all been seen on the school premises and identified by several people. Each boy admitted some responsibility for the damage caused.

Lance: 'We started this game – it was Brett's idea – throwing stones over the school building into the field next door. We didn't actually break the windows. We just cracked them.

'Greg smashed the door. He was just showing off on his bike.

'Anyway, there's nothing to do here. This place is dead.'

Brett: 'We were just having a laugh. We didn't know we had done any damage until the police came.

'It must have been Greg who broke the windows because he's a useless thrower.'

Greg: 'I rode into the door on my bike. The brakes just failed. But I didn't break the windows. I only threw a couple of stones. I told them it was stupid.

'Lance set the bin on fire with his fags. Brett and I don't smoke.'

In the space of about an hour, the three boys caused more than £1,800 worth of damage.

? Questions

1 What do you think are the important facts in this case – as far as the law is concerned?

2 How would you share out the responsibility for what happened? Are the three boys equally responsible? Explain the reasons behind your thinking.

What next?

There is no doubt that Lance and his friends gave the school an expensive repair bill. What should happen to them now? Should they be punished? Or should they be treated in some other way?

Here are the alternatives:

Deterrent

Do something that makes sure the boys are put off doing the same thing again.

Do nothing

Take no further action.

Punishment

Perhaps a fine, or some kind of penalty that punishes the boys for what they have done.

Rehabilitation

Make the boys understand that what they did was wrong, so that they won't do it again.

Reparation

This involves the boys doing something to make up for or to repair the damage they have done.

Reprimand

A strict telling off.

3 Would you reject any of these alternatives straightaway? Are there any that you feel are definitely not the right way to deal with this case?

4 Which of the alternatives do you think are most appropriate? You may choose more than one. Explain the thinking behind your answer.

Decision

The police gave both Brett and Greg a **reprimand**, as this was the first time they had been in trouble.

But Lance had done this kind of thing once before, and the police decided to give him a **final warning**. Lance was also asked by the Youth Offending Team if he would be prepared to meet those affected by what he did. Lance agreed.

KeyWords

Final warning

Instead of sending someone to court, the police give that person one last warning.

Reprimand

A formal telling off, by a senior police officer, designed to make sure that the young person realises that what they did was wrong and persuade them not to commit a similar offence again. A person given a reprimand or final warning must admit responsibility for the crime.

Back to school

Exactly two weeks after the incident had taken place, Lance and his parents walked into his old primary school and were shown into the head teacher's office. Also present were the school's chair of governors, the school caretaker and a police officer.

Counting the cost

The police officer present introduced everyone, and asked Mrs Carpenter, the head teacher, if she would like to speak first.

Mrs Carpenter said that she was shocked when she saw the damage that had been done. She said that she was also very hurt because it involved three of her ex-pupils.

Mr Bridges, the caretaker, explained that he had found it very difficult to mend the door and that it took more than a week to get the windows replaced. He said that the fire in the bin had made a real mess and that he had felt very angry that the school that he tried to maintain had been

Mrs Khan, the chair of governors, told Lance that the repair bill would come to £1,890. Last term, hoping to save money, the school had decided to cancel its insurance policy covering this kind of damage. The cost of the repairs would therefore have to come from the budget for books and other school materials.

Finally, Lance's mum said that she was upset about having to go to the police station. She was also worried about his sister, Amy, who was in Year 5 at the school. The previous week, Amy had come home in tears because people were picking on her for the damage caused by her brother and his friends.

As he heard about the difficulties his sister was facing, Lance began to cry. The police officer suggested a short break.

When everyone returned, Lance was asked if there was anything he would like to say or do to make up for the damage caused.

I promise to be good
signed Lance

1 Who do you think are the victims in this case? Try to explain how they have each been affected.

2 Why do you think Lance was asked to meet Mrs Carpenter and other people connected with the school? What were the police trying to achieve?

3 Do you think Lance was treated fairly? Do you think Mrs Khan should have asked Lance and his parents to pay for the damage?

Lance said he was sorry for the trouble that he had caused his family and the damage that he had caused to the school building.

Promise

Mrs Carpenter asked for a written promise from Lance saying that he would not come on to school property again without good reason. Mrs Khan knew that Lance's family had very little money and did not ask either Lance or his mother to pay anything towards the cost of the damage.

HEAD TEACHER

If Lance commits another offence he will be sent to court for trial. If he is found guilty, his failure to follow his final warning may count against him.

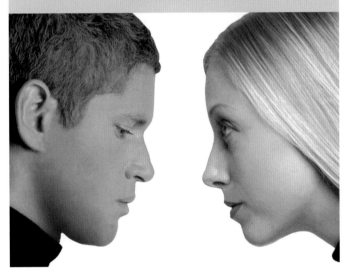

Victims and offenders

The idea of bringing together victims and offenders is quite new. It takes a long time to organise, but is used now in all kinds of cases. It is never forced on people and both sides must agree to meet. It is not an alternative to punishment.

4 What do you think are the advantages and disadvantages of arranging meetings between victims and offenders?

A helping hand

the **cancer** research campaign

In this unit we ask some questions about charities and the way in which we support them.

Reasons for giving

'I wanted to do something before going to university and I applied to go on a trekking adventure in Kenya. I did a sponsored walk, wrote to local businesses, and organised some discos in the village where I live, raising £2,500. This covered the cost of my trip and left enough for a donation to Barnardo's, the **charity** that organised the event.'
Michelle, aged 21.

'I watched the films shown on Comic Relief about their work in Africa. I was really moved by what I saw and rang through with a £25 donation.'
John, aged 44.

'I work in our local Oxfam shop. I was lonely after my husband died, and it helps me to meet people. I feel I'm supporting a good cause.'
Dorothy, aged 67.

'Once a term, we have a non-uniform day. Everyone at school has to give 50p for charity if they want to come to school in ordinary clothes.'
Ben, aged 14.

'Three years ago I started to feel dizzy and sick. I went to the doctor and he told me that I had a tumour on the brain. I had a big operation, followed by a lot of treatment. With help from my family and friends and the hospital, I made a full recovery. Now I want to help other people in the same position. I've just done a sponsored swim, raising £500 for cancer research.'
Natalie, aged 17.

'My mum lives with my son and me. She's elderly and we don't have much space, but you can't leave her on her own – not when she's family.'
Irene, aged 36.

? Questions

1 Look at what each of these people have said and suggest what you think is their main reason for helping or supporting others.

2 Are any of these reasons better than others? If you feel they are, try to explain what you mean.

Jackpot!

In January 2000, Ray and Barbara Wragg from Sheffield won the National Lottery. They bought a larger house and a new car, and gave some money to their children, but soon decided that the £7.6m they had left over was too much money for two people. Since 2000 they have been giving their money away, and so far more than £6m has been donated to local charities and other good causes.

3 How would you describe Mr and Mrs Wragg's decision to give away most of their money? Wise? Foolish? Generous?

4 Would you agree that anyone with more than £7 million *ought* to give some of their money to charity?

5 Do rich, powerful or successful people have a greater duty to help others? Give reasons for your answer.

6 What do you think are good reasons on the list opposite? What are the bad reasons? Can you explain why these are bad?

7 How do you normally deal with this situation?

Deciding for the best

You're walking through town on a Saturday afternoon and you're stopped by a young man, aged about 20, asking if you could spare any change for a cup of tea. He looks scruffy, his clothes are dirty and you can smell alcohol on his breath. What do you do?

Here are some reasons why you might decide to help him:

- He must be desperate if he has to stop people in the street.
- This could be me one day.
- He looks ill. I should help him.
- If I give him some money, he'll leave me alone.

... and some reasons why you might decide not to:

- I don't have 20p.
- If I give him any money, he'll only spend it on drink or drugs.
- Why should I help him? He's only got himself to blame.
- It's just a con. I don't think he is poor at all.
- People will look at me as I do it.

KeyWords

Charity
An organisation set up to provide help or raise money for a particular group in the community.

A helping hand

Charities

Going up

In 2007, there were just over 190,000 registered charities in Britain – more than in any other country in the world. About 5,000 new charities are registered each year.

Most charities are very small – only five per cent employ paid staff – but some are large and very well known.

RSPCA   GREENPEACE   Barnard

Questions

1 Draw up a list of as many charities as you can think of.

2 Alongside the name of each charity, make a note of the kind of work that you think they do.

Household names

In your list you might have mentioned the children's charity Barnardo's, Oxfam, which helps to relieve poverty, or the RSPCA, which works to prevent cruelty to animals.

Oxfam

Barnardo's
GIVING CHILDREN BACK THEIR FUTURE

Each of these charities is a large, well-known organisation. The RSPCA, for example, provides help and treatment to thousands of animals and deals with millions of pounds every year.

In this way, they are just like companies making computers or chocolate but, unlike Compaq or Cadbury, charities are not in business to make profits for people who have put money into the company. All the money that charities receive must be put back into their work.

Becoming a charity allows an organisation to keep more of its money. It doesn't have to pay tax on the money that it receives and sometimes receives special discounts, particularly on costs such as council tax.

3 The information in the law section on page 45 gives the legal definition of a charity. Look again at your list and use this information to check whether each of the organisations that you wrote down fits this definition.

4 If some of those on your list appear not to be charities, try to explain why.

The trouble with politics

Organisations such as Amnesty International and Greenpeace are often thought of as charities because, in many people's minds, they do good work.

Amnesty campaigns against torture and tries to obtain the release of people who they feel have been jailed for political reasons. Greenpeace tries to prevent further damage to the environment.

However, as far as the law is concerned, neither of these organisations is a charity because they both take part in political activities.

Charities have to help the public as a whole. Political views are a matter of opinion. They cannot be guaranteed to be a help or benefit to the community.

Not straightforward

Perhaps surprisingly, one of the richest charities in Britain is Eton College, the public school in Berkshire, which counts royal princes among its students. Although most students who attend are from wealthy backgrounds, schools like Eton College qualify as charities because they are places of education.

Good causes?

In Britain, we give more money to animal charities than we give to charities that help the disabled. In 2000, an elderly woman left £7 million to a charity for dogs. A charity for hamsters reportedly has funds of nearly £10 million.

> **5** 'It's not right to give animals huge amounts of money when human beings are suffering in so many ways.' What arguments can you think of in favour of and against this point of view?

The law

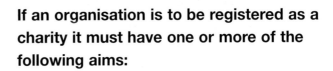

If an organisation is to be registered as a charity it must have one or more of the following aims:

- to relieve the poor, the sick, the handicapped or the aged
- to advance education
- to advance religion
- to provide a benefit to the community.

A charity must help the public as a whole, and not individuals or small groups of people. It must not be political, for example, by campaigning to change the law.

Rich and poor

In this unit we look at ways of trying to reduce the differences between rich and poor countries and ask who has responsibility to do something about this.

Making a difference

School days

Mark Orchard, a builder from Somerset, and his family went on holiday to Kenya. They stayed at the Turtle Bay Beach Club, a large, modern, air-conditioned hotel, with a swimming pool and the most up-to-date facilities.

During his stay, Mark became friendly with Geoffrey Chege, one of the hotel workers. One day, Geoffrey took Mark to visit the school in Dabaso, the village where he lived. There were 90 children in each class, and no proper school building. In Kenya, it is the responsibility of parents and teachers to build new classrooms for their school, but the people of Dabaso were too poor to raise the money required.

Back in England, Mark told his workmates about what he had seen. 'If *we* could get the money and materials,' he said, 'we could construct a new school building for them.'

Mark raised the money through friends and the people he worked with, and later that year went back to Dabaso with four of his mates. Rising at 5a.m. each day, they worked into the night. There was no electricity or running water in the village and the heat was a major problem, but in three weeks they had finished the building.

The villagers repaid the five men by making them tribal elders. It was the highest honour they could give.

Continued fund-raising has helped to provide Dabaso with a library and medical centre. The village is also now twinned with Hutton in Somerset.

? Questions

1 What do you think was most remarkable about what was done by Mark and his friends?

2 Many people from rich countries spend their holidays in parts of the world, like Kenya, where there is a great deal of poverty. What is your opinion of this? Should these holidays be encouraged or discouraged?

Target 2015

In the mid-1990s, many governments throughout the world, including Britain, agreed to try to cut world poverty by a half by the year 2015.

This is a huge task and everyone knows how difficult it will be.

One of the questions that countries have to decide is how they will achieve this. Here are some of the things that could be done.

- **Money**
Raise the amount of money given by richer countries to help with famines and other emergencies.

- **Help with basics**
Help poorer countries to improve their water supply, install electricity and build better roads.

- **Training**
Give free advice and training to introduce new industries and more modern methods of production.

- **Schools and hospitals**
Provide help for the long-term future by giving money for education and health.

- **Trade**
Make it easier for poorer countries to sell their goods in Britain and other wealthy countries.

- **Environment**
Help with the replanting of trees in those areas where forests have been cut down to create farmland and for the sale of timber. This will reverse damage to the land, help stop the extinction of certain species and reduce some of the effects of climate change.

- **Equality for women**
Give women the same rights as men in education, work and politics. This will improve people's health and standard of living, and will make it more likely that people will have smaller families.

3 Look through each of these points. Are there any that you do not agree with and would reject? If there are, try to explain why.

4 Which three suggestions would you put into practice first? Explain why.

5 Is there anything that individuals (rather than governments) should do to reduce the amount of poverty in the world? If so, what do you feel it is?

6 Should we ever attach conditions to money that we give to poorer countries? (For example, that they spend less on their army, that they don't damage the environment, or that undemocratic countries improve the way their country is run?)

Rich and poor

A tale of two cities

Juba

'Juba is a large town in southern Sudan, where I met Agnes and Richard. They had a two-year-old child, Grace, who was suffering from malaria, a fever carried by mosquitoes.

"We had to find the money to pay for the drugs that Grace needed," said Agnes. "We spent a day going round our friends and relatives asking them for help. We needed to find four hundred Sudanese dinar to cover the cost of Grace's treatment."

'When they had raised enough cash, they walked for three hours to the hospital. Richard raced ahead and was standing at the hospital gate, with a doctor, as Agnes arrived carrying their tiny child. But Grace died in her mother's arms at the hospital gate. Four hundred dinar is 96p.'

Nick Weston, charity worker.

Leeds

'I remember the night my son was diagnosed with cancer. I was helping him with his homework and noticed a swelling on the side of his neck. I rang the doctor, who told me to bring Paul round as soon as possible. After a brief examination, she phoned the hospital and I took Paul there in the car straightaway. Paul was in hospital for ten days. The doctors knew what the problem was, but wanted time to work out the exact dosage of drugs that he needed. Paul's treatment consisted of eight different tablets, three times a day. Once a fortnight he went back into hospital for six or seven other drugs, given to him through an injection or on a drip. One day I asked the doctor how much they cost. The injection that he was giving at the moment, the doctor said, cost £17. Paul is now fully recovered.'

Robert James, electrician.

1 What are the similarities and the differences in the stories on page 48?

2 What do you think are the reasons for or causes of these differences?

3 What are the effects of poverty on individuals and families?

4 Why don't we just share out our wealth more evenly?

The big picture

A world problem

According to the United Nations, about 25,000 people die each day from hunger or from illnesses associated with this. Four out of ten people living in Africa, south of the Sahara, live in extreme poverty.

Currently a person born in the African country of Malawi can expect to live on average for about 40 years. Compare that with a life expectancy in Britain of 81 for women and 76 for men.

Not all bad news

Some countries are managing to improve the lives of their people.

Many more now have a safe water supply in comparison to 20 years ago. More children are able to go to primary school than ever before.

There are fewer children who are seriously underweight and the number living in poverty in certain countries, such as China, has fallen greatly over the last ten years.

5 What do you think are the consequences of such a large number of people in the world living in poverty?

6 Do any of these consequences affect us here in Britain? If you think they do, try to explain how.

7 Does it matter that there is such a wide difference in the standard of living between the rich and the poor? If you believe it does, try to explain why.

Wasting away

In this unit we ask how we should be dealing with the increasing amount of waste that we produce in our society.

Explosive mixture

At 6.30a.m, Mr and Mrs Thompson and their son Colin were still fast asleep in their bungalow. Suddenly, with no warning, there was a huge explosion.

'The first thing I was aware of was a flying sensation, and then darkness,' said Mr Thompson. Mr Thompson was badly injured. He had been blown across the room and buried under a pile of rubble. Colin was found beneath the floorboards and Mrs Thompson was left looking at the sky through a hole in the roof.

The Thompsons' house, their car and all their other possessions were completely destroyed.

The family lived in the village of Loscoe in Derbyshire. Close to their estate was an old clay pit that had been used as a dump for rubble and household waste. When the pit was full it was left to settle. It was then covered with a thick layer of soil.

As some kinds of waste decompose, they produce a gas called methane, which is very explosive. Methane from the clay pit collected underneath the floor of the Thompsons' bungalow. On the morning in question, the central heating automatically switched on at 6.30a.m, and the results were shattering.

? Questions

1 Who do you think had some responsibility for the damage and injuries suffered by the Thompsons?

2 Who should have responsibility for safely disposing of our rubbish?

Down in the dumps

After the explosion in Loscoe, which happened in 1986, laws were passed to try to make sure that a similar build-up of gas could not take place at the many other tips dotted around the country.

Although there are now very strict rules about the ways in which waste tips must be managed, one big problem hasn't gone away: what do we do with all our rubbish?

Waste disposal route

About 30 million tonnes of household waste is collected in the UK every year – that's about 537kg or half a tonne per person.

A little over 20 per cent of this is recycled. Just under ten per cent is used to produce energy, and 70 per cent is buried in the ground.

• Landfill
Waste is put into large pits or holes, such as disused mines or quarries. Landfill keeps the rubbish out of sight, but there are worries that dangerous chemicals from the waste can seep through the rocks into the water supply. Laws now state what can and cannot be placed in landfill sites and what must be done to prevent leakage from the tip. There are concerns about a health risk to those living near landfill sites.

We are running out of landfill sites. Over the next 15 years Britain is required, under European law, to reduce significantly the amount of waste sent for landfill.

• Burning
Burning rubbish in specially built incinerators gets rid of waste without some of the problems of landfill. The heat produced is used to generate electricity.

People worry that dangerous gases may be released from these incinerators.

• Recycle
Paper, glass and metal can all be recycled and used again, saving valuable resources. Recycling also avoids some of the problems of landfill and burning.

However, some people argue that the environment is damaged more by collecting, transporting and recycling paper than burning it in a specially built incinerator.

---

3 How do you think the kind of waste that we produce today compares with the situation in the past? How has it changed over the last a) 5 years b) 100 years c) 1000 years?

4 Bury, burn and recycle are three methods of dealing with rubbish. Can you think of any ways of *reducing* the amount of waste that we produce?

Wasting away

Throwaway society

Save!

This book was written on a two-year-old computer. By today's standards it is already out of date, with faster models being developed all the time. Together the computer and screen contain about seven kilos of glass and 35 different metals and elements, some of which are hazardous.

Computers are being so quickly replaced that about 50 million tonnes of old PCs are thrown away each year.

In the bin

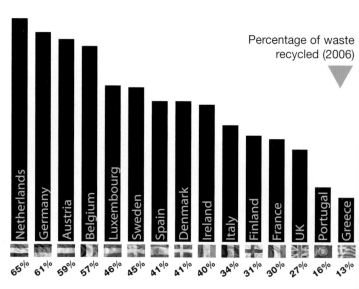

Figures from Open University, 2006

Other Waste

Dust & Ash 3%

Other 15%

Sanitary 10%

Paper & Card 8%

Glass 4%

Metal 5%

Household Waste

Plastics 18%

Kitchen & Garden Waste 36%

Biodegradable Waste

Clothes 1%

How do we compare?

Recycling rates in Britain have improved greatly in recent years, but we still recycle less of our rubbish than many other European countries.

THINK! Look at the figures in the pie chart showing the type of waste that we place in our bins at home. Which items would it be possible to a) re-use and b) recycle? Could we cut down on any of this waste?

Difficulties

Until the 1970s in Britain, most of the bottles in which drinks were sold were made of glass and were returnable. However, in 1971, the drinks company Schweppes decided that it would no longer accept returned bottles.

Friends of the Earth, the environmental pressure group, launched a big campaign against this, dumping large numbers of the new non-returnable bottles on the doorstep of Schweppes' headquarters in London.

Percentage of waste recycled (2006)

Country	%
Netherlands	65%
Germany	61%
Austria	59%
Belgium	57%
Luxembourg	46%
Sweden	45%
Spain	41%
Denmark	41%
Ireland	40%
Italy	34%
Finland	31%
France	30%
UK	27%
Portugal	16%
Greece	13%

Over the last 35 years, the situation has become worse, rather than better. Today, almost all the packaging in which we buy things (except glass milk bottles) is non-returnable. Most of it, as we have seen, is thrown away.

Action!

The Government has said that Britain's rate of recycling must improve. It has a target of recycling 50 per cent of household waste by 2020.

But how can we increase our rate of recycling? Here are some ideas that have been suggested and tried.

• Charge householders for the amount of non-recyclable rubbish they put out for collection. The more they leave, the more they pay. *This system has been introduced in Ireland.*

• Fine householders who do not sort out all their recyclable rubbish.

• Have stricter laws preventing companies from selling products with excessive packaging.

• Either ban the sale of plastic bags or require shops to charge 20p for each one a customer uses. *A tax on plastic carriers was introduced in Ireland in 2002. Plastic bags are banned in a number of African and Asian countries, e.g. Bangladesh.*

• Place a charge of 15–20p on all drinks sold in cans, plastic or glass bottles, which can be reclaimed when the container is returned. *This kind of system has been run for some time in Germany, Sweden and Switzerland.*

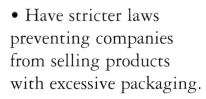

? Questions

1 Look at each idea for improving recycling and draw up a list of advantages and disadvantages for each one.

2 Do you have any other ideas yourself? Again, write down what you think would be the advantages and disadvantages.

3 Now put yourself in the position of the Government. Which three, out of all the ideas you have considered, would be most effective?

KeyWords

Biodegradable
Can decompose naturally into a harmless substance.

Recycle
Breaking something down to its raw materials and using this to make the same or a new product. Books and magazines are often made from recycled paper.

Re-use
Using something again for the same purpose.

Global warming

In this unit we consider whether any action should be taken as a result of changes in our climate.

All change

Melting moments

In the summer of 2000, a group of American tourists took their holiday on a huge Russian icebreaker. Their aim was to travel as far north as they could, cutting through the ice to reach the North Pole.

When their instruments showed that they were at 90 degrees north and had reached the Pole, they did not see the wide-open frozen landscape that they had expected. Instead, their gaze fell upon large stretches of open water. The nearest section of ice thick enough for the group to get off the ship and stand upon was six miles away.

There is no land at the North Pole. It lies in a frozen sea – the Arctic Ocean. A small amount of open water is not unusual, but the Russian captain of the vessel said that he had made the journey to the Pole ten times and had never before come across an open sea.

Scientists have known for many years that the ice caps over both the North and South Poles are melting. Over the past 50 years the ice cover over the area is thought to have shrunk by about 45 per cent.

? Questions ? ? ?

1   What would you think may be some of the effects of the ice melting at the North Pole?

What's going on?

- **Getting warmer** Over the last hundred years there have been fewer frosts and more heat waves in many parts of the world.

Five of the warmest years on record in Britain have occurred this century, and 2006 was the warmest ever recorded. Spring temperatures in 2007 were 0.2°C higher than the previous record of 1945.

- **Rainy days** The summer of 2007 was, for some parts of Britain, the wettest on record. At the same time, millions of people in India and Bangladesh were driven from their homes because of extensive flooding that followed heavier than usual monsoon rain.

The greenhouse effect

The atmosphere of the earth is warmed by energy from the sun. Much of this heat is reflected back into space, but some is trapped inside a layer of gases, which surrounds the earth. This is called the greenhouse effect, and stops the earth from cooling down too quickly. If the layer did not exist, a huge amount of heat would be lost and temperatures would fall by about 30°C.

The main gases creating the greenhouse effect are water vapour, carbon dioxide, methane and nitrous oxide, all of which occur naturally.

Since the beginning of the 19th century, human activities, such as the burning of fossil fuels (coal, gas and oil) for heating and power, have released large amounts of carbon dioxide into the atmosphere. As a result, levels of the gas have risen by about 30 per cent over the last 200 years.

Most scientists agree that this has raised the temperature of our atmosphere.

Proving the link

Many believe that there is a direct link between the increase in greenhouse gases and the change in our climate.

However, not all scientists will say with *certainty* that the two are connected. The head of the weather service in Britain has said that severe storms and floods are not proof of global warming.

Climate change over long periods of time is quite normal. There is evidence that a mini 'ice age' began in Europe about 500 years ago. Pictures of a frozen River

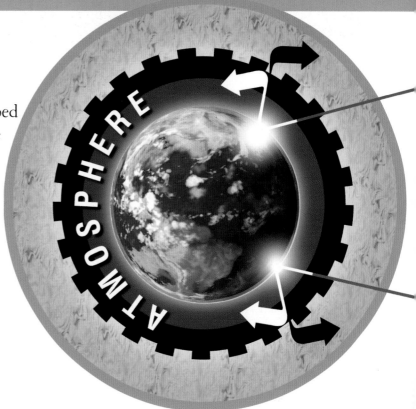

Thames, painted in the 1700s, show that winters in England were probably much colder then than they are now.

The questions facing governments throughout the world are whether to take action to try to reduce global warming and, if action is taken, what it should be.

2 Do you think that action should be taken to reduce levels of greenhouse gases in our atmosphere? If so, who has responsibility for this?

3 If governments do decide to try to reduce global warming, what kinds of things will they have to do? What sorts of changes may have to be made? How will they affect our lives in the future?

Global warming

Taking action

The Kyoto agreement

In 1997, at a conference in the Japanese city of Kyoto, 118 countries signed what has become known as the Kyoto agreement. It didn't come into force until 2005, but now has the support of more than 170 states.

It is part of a **United Nations** programme designed to reduce levels of carbon dioxide and other greenhouse gases in the atmosphere.

Under the Kyoto agreement, **developed countries**, such as Canada, Russia, Japan, Britain and other European states, have promised that by 2008–2012 they will have cut the amount of greenhouse gases they release into the atmosphere by five per cent below 1990 levels. This is a legal agreement under international law, and countries that fail to meet their targets may have to pay a financial penalty and make further reductions from 2012.

Under the treaty, **developing countries**, such as India, China, and states in Africa and South America, have a responsibility to reduce emissions, but do not have the same targets as developed countries. This is because historically most pollution has originated in developed countries.

Broken promise?

When the original Kyoto agreement was drawn up in 1997, it had the support of Bill Clinton, then president of the United States. In 2000, America had a new president, George W Bush, and in early 2001 President Bush announced that the United States would no longer support the Kyoto agreement.

Explaining the reasons for his decision, Mr Bush said that the agreement would harm the US economy and put people out of work. He said that the treaty was unfair to the US and other developed countries as developing countries were not bound to reduce their emissions in the same way.

Mr Bush said it would be better for a cut in greenhouse gases to be made through voluntary agreements and the development of new energy-saving technology.

? Questions

1 Did Mr Bush have the right to alter an agreement his country had already made? Try to explain your reasoning.

2 Mr Bush said that developing countries should also be required to reduce the levels of greenhouse gases they produce. Do you agree with this?

Predictions for the future

It is very difficult to predict the weather accurately, but many scientists now believe that over the next 100 years increased levels of greenhouse gases are likely to mean that:

- temperatures over land will rise by between 2°C and 4°C
- seas will generally become warmer
- sea levels will rise in many parts of the world
- there will be less ice covering high mountain and polar regions
- the climate in many parts of the world will change.

3 Look again at each of the changes that scientists believe will take place if temperatures continue to rise over the next 100 years, and try to think of a consequence or effect of each one.

4 On balance, do you feel these changes are for the better or the worse? Try to explain your view.

5 Some people have argued that there is little point in having the Kyoto agreement if it does not include the US – a country that emits more greenhouse gases than any other. How should Britain and other European countries respond to this? What should and shouldn't they do?

Mail storm

Mr Bush was criticised heavily for his decision. At one stage, more than 1,000 email messages an hour were being sent to  his office from people all over the world. It was reported that the White House server had crashed twice under the strain.

KeyWords

Developed countries
Countries where most of the population has a relatively high standard of living, in comparison with people in the world as a whole.

Developing countries
Countries that are in the process of modernisation, but where people generally have a relatively low standard of living.

United Nations
An organisation to which almost every state belongs. Its main aim is to keep world peace.

Animals matter

In this unit we look at some questions about the way in which we should treat animals.

Cruelty to animals

For life

Ken bought Benje, a large puppy, as a present for his wife, Maria. Ken's work often took him abroad. He thought the dog would be company for his wife while he was away.

It wasn't long before he realised that he had made a mistake. Maria found it difficult to look after the fast-growing dog and she was worried for the safety of their daughter, Alicia, who was a year old.

They had had Benje for about six months when Maria told Ken that he would have to get rid of the dog. Ken could see her point. The dog was becoming a handful. Their flat in Brighton was too small for such a large animal. Maria was planning to go back to work. It wouldn't be fair to leave the dog at home all day.

Ken decided that the quickest thing to do would be to drive out into the countryside and leave Benje on the side of the road. Ken let Benje jump out of the car and then drove off. He thought that someone might find the dog and look after him.

Three weeks later, a neighbour rang to say that Benje was in the street outside. The dog had managed to find his way home.

The same evening, around 11p.m, Ken took Benje for a walk along the sea front. He tied Benje by his lead to some railings, and left him. The next morning Benje was found hanging from the railings.

? Questions

1 Most people would probably feel that Ken had made a number of mistakes. What do you think they are?

2 Did Ken break the law? If so, how?

3 If you feel that Ken broke the law, how should he be dealt with by the courts?

The protection of animals

There are more than 70 laws that protect animals in some way.

The first law specially designed to do this was passed in 1822. It made it an offence 'to beat, abuse or ill-treat any horse, mare, gelding, ass, ox, cow, heifer, steer, sheep or other cattle.'

In 1835, it became an offence to treat a dog cruelly and to keep any animals without food. In the same year, bull-baiting, bear-baiting and cockfighting were also outlawed.

Seabirds were the first British *wild* animals to be protected by law. This was because, by hovering over shoals of fish, they guided fishing boats towards the best catches.

In the 1860s and 1870s, many people protested against the ways in which animals were treated in research. The first law controlling this was passed in 1876.

There have been many further changes in the law. The shooting of pigeons specially bred in captivity was banned in 1921. Laws protecting badgers and seals were passed in the 1970s, and in 1996 it became an offence to inflict suffering on any wild animal. The testing of cosmetics on animals has been banned in the UK since 1997.

Use or abuse?

The British have a reputation for being kind to animals. However, some people feel that there is still too much cruelty.

Here are some of the ways in which we use animals today that are not against the law:

• for scientific research • as a source of food • for work • in sport • for hunting and shooting • for pleasure.

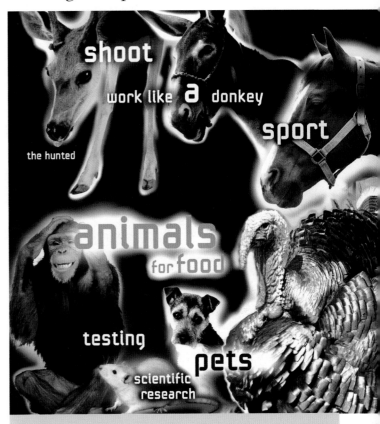

4 Briefly describe how we use animals in each of the ways listed.

5 Are animals used in any way that you dislike or are uncomfortable with? Explain what they are and why you feel as you do.

The law

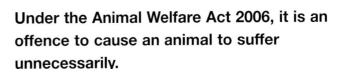

Under the Animal Welfare Act 2006, it is an offence to cause an animal to suffer unnecessarily.

Anyone who is found guilty of being cruel to an animal or not looking after its welfare can be banned from owning animals, be fined up to £20,000 and/or be sent to prison.

chicken ('tʃikin) n 1. a domestic fowl now reared for its meat and eggs. 2. a pecking, scratching, perching creature. For healthy growth needs space to flap its wings and to take dust baths to clean its feathers. 3. evolved from the Red Jungle Fowl of Thailand. 4. first domesticated about 8,000 years ago and spread to Europe via China, India and Egypt. 5. in Britain was originally bred mainly for sport. The rearing of chickens on a large scale began in the 1920s and steadily grew for the remainder of the century.

Chicken tonight

Battery life

Most of the eggs eaten by people in Britain are from hens kept in cages, known as batteries. The chickens stand on a wire floor, with up to five birds in each cage. With a space of about 23 x 23cm (a bit larger than the size of an A4 sheet of paper) available for each hen, there is not enough room for the birds to walk and stretch their wings. The structure of the cage prevents the birds from pecking on the ground for food, perching or building a nest.

Cheap

Battery farming enables egg farmers to produce eggs at a lower price than by other methods. Half a dozen free-range eggs cost about 10p more than eggs laid by battery hens.

Change the batteries

In 1999, agricultural ministers in the **European Union** ruled that from 2012 hens could no longer be kept in cages. However, some people now wish to delay the ban or drop it completely.

A rare treat

If you ask anyone over the age of 50 about the food they used to eat at home when they were young, they will probably say that they had chicken only two or three times a year. In the 1960s, it was an expensive luxury.

> **!** THINK! How important to you are the conditions in which laying hens are kept?
>
> Are you prepared to pay more for eggs from birds reared in a better environment?

Today

More chicken is eaten in Britain today than at probably any other time in history. In 2005, 864 million birds were reared and killed in Britain – to be eaten roasted, grilled or fried.

Unless they are free-range birds, broilers (as they are known) spend their entire life in a building with no windows, but with artificial light controlled to go on and off automatically.

Broilers are different from laying hens and are often raised with up to 25,000 other birds in a building. Conditions are very crowded. Birds each have a space roughly equal to that covered by this open book. Many young chickens (about seven per cent) die before they are ready to be slaughtered.

Those that survive, rapidly put on weight. Their diet is designed to produce as much flesh as possible, particularly on the breast. As a result, the birds are often very overweight in relation to the strength and size of their muscles and bones. They have difficulty in moving and it is likely that many of the chickens are in a great deal of pain.

Forty-two days after they are hatched, the birds are killed.

? Questions

1 What are the arguments for allowing birds to be treated like this? What are the arguments against? Which arguments do you feel are stronger?

2 The law states that it is an offence to cause an animal to suffer unnecessarily. However, all animals used for human consumption probably suffer at some time in their lives. How much suffering should the law allow?

3 Who do you think has responsibility for chickens being kept in this way? Is it just one group of people, or do others also share responsibility? Does anyone have responsibility to change the way in which we obtain our meat?

KeyWords

European Union
A group of 27 European countries, of which Britain is one, which between them make certain laws that apply to all member states. These laws tend to concentrate on certain areas of life, in particular trade, work, farming, transport and the environment.

Animals matter

Testing times

Dog days

Digger is a 16-week-old beagle. He's owned by a company that carries out experiments on animals – testing the safety of new drugs and other substances that will be used by human beings.

Digger spends most of the day in a pen, just over 2 metres x 2 metres in size. The gate of the pen is sometimes left open, so he can mix with other dogs being used in the same test. Digger is fed twice a day and exercised in the laboratory corridor. Every hour, a technician checks for signs of problems among the dogs.

Both of Digger's meals are dosed with the substance he is testing. It could be a drug designed to treat heart disease, a fertiliser that farmers will spread on the land, or a new colouring for food. Samples of Digger's urine and faeces are collected for analysis and once a week he is weighed and given a blood test. When he is about a year old, Digger will be killed. His organs will be carefully analysed to check the effect of the substance that is being tested.

Safety first

People have a right to expect things that they buy to be absolutely safe. In order to protect themselves from being taken to court for making something dangerous or harmful, companies take time to check that their products are as safe as possible, before putting them on sale.

If the product is to be used in the manufacture of food or is likely to come into direct contact with animals or human beings, the company may decide to test it on animals. In fact, if it is a medicine, it *must* be tested on animals before being trialled by humans and used by the general public.

Pain and suffering

People who disapprove of using animals in scientific research believe that it is wrong to inflict pain on animals deliberately. They also argue that using animals to predict the safety of a drug or a

food additive for humans is not always accurate. Different species can react differently to the same substance.

Permission

When an organisation wants to use animals for research, it must apply for permission to do so from the Home Office, the government department with responsibility for overseeing the tests.

The Home Office will look at the aims of the experiment and how it will be carried out. It should check that there is a *need* for the test and that as few animals as possible are used. The experiment should also be designed to cause animals the minimum amount of distress.

Figures

In 2006, licences were given for just over 3 million animal experiments to take place in Britain. More than 90 per cent of these were with mice, rats and fish. Dogs, cats and monkeys were used in about 12,000 experiments.

In about 38 per cent of the experiments, animals were given some kind of anaesthetic to ease the pain.

In Britain, we earn a great deal of money from the research carried out using animals. It is also big business in many other parts of the world. In the United States, for example, more than 30 million animal experiments take place each year.

? Questions

1 What are the arguments in favour of using animals for scientific research? What are the arguments against? What position do you take on using animals in scientific tests?

2 Would you favour a change in the law or would you leave things as they are? Try to give a reason for your answer.

The law

People who use animals in scientific research must obtain a special licence for the procedure that they want to carry out. An experiment using animals will be allowed if it helps to:

- prevent, treat or diagnose disease in animals, plants or humans
- understand the workings of animals, plants or humans
- protect the environment
- advance scientific knowledge
- breed animals for scientific use
- investigate crime.

A licence will also be granted to use animals for educational research – but not in schools.

The price of air travel

In this unit we look at some of the advantages and disadvantages of air travel and the action some people are taking in response to airport expansion.

Getaway

On the day on which this section was written, a quick search on the internet found a return flight from London to Stockholm (the capital of Sweden), a distance of almost 1,800 miles or 2,800 km, for 2 pence, plus £39.23 airport taxes.

Cheap fares make travelling by air very attractive. It is possible to spend a weekend in Venice, in Italy, for the price of a short break in England or Wales.

Many people are also choosing to fly to places in the UK rather than travel by rail. It is often cheaper and faster.

? Questions

1 Yan needs to travel from London to Glasgow to visit her parents. She plans to stay one night, and return the following day.

   She checks the fares, and this is what she finds:

   Plane £20.00 return
   journey time 1 hour 15 mins

   Train £97.20 return
   journey time 5 hours 30 mins

   Coach £30.00 return
   journey time 8–10 hours

   a) What are the advantages and disadvantages of each form of travel?

   b) Which ticket would you recommend she buys?

2 Draw up a list of some of the possible effects of so many more people travelling by air.

3 Now sort your list of effects into good effects and bad effects.

Air miles

People throughout the world are flying more often to more destinations than ever before. Official statistics predict that between 2005 and 2030, the number of UK air passengers will rise from 229 million to 500 million per year.

Pollution and climate change

Passenger jets can move people long distances quickly, but are also a major source of pollution. Aircraft use most fuel when taking off and landing. This means that short flights, such as those within Britain and to nearby cities in Europe, are the least efficient. One short flight produces as much carbon dioxide as the average car emits in a year.

Air travel is the fastest-growing source of greenhouse gases. Many believe that there is a direct link between greenhouse gases and the change in our climate.

A green tax

At present, unlike road users, airlines do not pay tax on the fuel they put in aeroplanes, nor is there any tax on the price of air tickets for journeys within the European Union – although we do pay tax on most other goods and services. Environmental campaigners, such as Friends of the Earth, say that passengers should pay for the environmental damage caused by their flight. They call for a new tax on aircraft fuel and tickets, which would raise the cost of each return journey by about £70.

Noise and disturbance

The increasing popularity of air travel means more airports are now being built. People living nearby are affected by greater road congestion and disturbance from night flights, which are now becoming more common.

A brake on air travel?

Some people feel that there should be less rather than more air travel. Others disagree, believing that greater air travel brings more benefits than problems.

Lee: 'People should travel by train, not air, and stop taking flights abroad for lots of holidays.'

Danny: 'People are entitled to enjoy themselves. If they want to go by plane, they should be able to do so.'

Lela: 'If we reduce the amount of air travel, businesses will suffer and tourists won't come here.'

Jody: 'We should not allow air travel to increase until we have sorted out the environmental problems that go with it.'

4 Look at the statements above and try to think of an argument for and against each one.

5 Which statements do you most and least agree with?

6 Do you think we should make air travel more expensive? Explain your views.

Heathrow Airport

Just not big enough

Heathrow Airport is situated on the outskirts of London. It is the busiest international airport in the world. Almost 70 million passengers use the airport each year – a large number travelling for work or business.

However, the popularity of air travel means that Heathrow is now working at full capacity. The British Airports Authority (BAA), which owns Heathrow, believes that Heathrow must become larger and argues that it cannot do so unless it has a third runway. This, says BAA, is the only way to make sure that Heathrow remains a world-class airport and that London continues to be the business and financial centre of Europe.

? Questions

1 A new runway at London Heathrow would allow the airport to handle up to 50 per cent more aircraft. What do you think are likely to be the advantages and disadvantages of this idea?

Support

It is planned that the new runway will be situated to the north of the existing airport, where the villages of Harmondsworth, Sipson and Harlington are now located. If the runway is built, around 700 houses and a school will need to be demolished. However, BAA argues that these losses will be offset by an extra £7 billion that will be brought to the area each year in jobs and commerce, rising to £30 billion by 2030.

The proposal also has the approval of the government, as long as the new development does not exceed set limits for air pollution and noise.

Objection

When the plans for the third runway were announced many local people were upset and angry. 'It's very demoralising,' said one resident, 'to think that a community is going to be wiped off the map.' Another said, 'How can it improve our life? Nobody considers the people involved.'

John Stewart, a member of a **pressure group** campaigning for quieter and safer conditions for those living near Heathrow, said the new runway would bring more noise and pollution. He added that many people living in London and the Home Counties would be affected by the new flight paths.

Others have objected to BAA's plan on grounds of the damage that they believe it would cause to the wider environment. Aviation, they argue, is the fastest-growing source of carbon emissions, and we should therefore be looking for ways to cut flights, not to increase them.

Action

When the plans for the new runway were announced, they were strongly criticised by local councils and residents' groups. At first each council was working on its own, but they soon decided that they would be more effective if they worked together. The 12 councils called themselves the 2M Group, representing two million Londoners, and decided to fight the plans in three ways:

- **Through the media** Using newspapers, radio, television and the internet, the councils try to influence local public opinion against airport expansion.

- **Influencing MPs** Arranging meetings with senior government figures and politicians to persuade them that existing plans should be changed.

- **Court action** Challenging the airport expansion in court, hoping that a judge will decide that certain parts of the plan are illegal.

Against the law

Not everyone, however, believes that this is enough. Some people, who have fought airport expansion for years without success, say that they plan to take part in direct action, even if it means breaking the law. This might include holding marches and demonstrations without police permission and preventing airport workers from going to work.

2 Draw up a list of what could be done by people who oppose the further expansion of Heathrow Airport.

3 Now list the strengths and weaknesses of each idea.

4 Is it ever right for protestors to break the law? Try to give reasons for your answer.

KeyWords

Pressure group
A group of people, or an organisation, formed to defend a particular interest or to campaign for change and to influence official policy.

Index and keywords

Index

A

Animals
– cruelty to **58–63**
– protection **59–63**
– and scientific research **62–63**
Arrest
– rights on **32–35**
Assault
– indecent **5, 7**

B

Bail **35–36**

C

Charities
– definition **43–45**
– giving to **42–43, 45**
Contraception **5, 8–9, 13**
Crime **14–41**
– causes of **28–29**
– cost of **24–25, 38–41**
– figures **22–23**
– and morality
14–15, 26–27, 30–31
– nature of **14–15, 18**
– reporting **22–23, 30–31**
– victims of **24–25, 40–41**
Crown Prosecutor **36–37**

D

Doctors
– confidentiality **8–9**

E

Environment
– climate change **54–57**
– recycling **51–53**
– waste disposal **50–53**
European Union **60–61**

F

Factory Farming **60–61**

L

Law
– changes in the **20–21**
– civil **19**
– criminal **19**
– and morality **14–15**
– unfair law **15**

M

Magistrates **36–37**
Morality **14–16**

N

National Lottery **42–43**

P

Parents
– and children
4, 7–9, 12, 34–35
– unmarried fathers **10–11**
– unmarried mothers **10–11, 13**
Police
– dealing with young
offenders **32–41**
Poverty **42–43, 46–49**
Pregnancy
– effects of **10–12**
– teenage **6, 8–13**
Punishment **37–41**

R

Rape **5**
Referral Order **37**

S

Sex
– age of consent **6–8**
– education **9–10, 12**
– in the media **5, 7**
– underage **6–13**
Sexually transmitted disease **11**
Solicitors **34–37**

T

Theft **16–17**

U

United Nations **56–57**

Y

Youth court **36–37**
Youth Offending Team **37**

Cross-referenced keywords

A

Affray **33**
Age of consent **7**
Arrest **33**

B

Bail **35**
Biodegradable **53**

C

Charity **43**
Child benefit **11**
Crown Prosecutor **37**

D

Developed countries **57**
Developing countries **57**
Duty solicitor **35**

E

European Union **61**

F

Final warning **39**

M

Magistrates **37**
Manslaughter **27**

P

Pressure Group **67**

R

Recycle **53**
Reprimand **39**
Re-use **53**

U

United Nations **57**

Y

Youth court **37**
Youth Offending Team **37**